the REAL AUSTRALIA

SUNSET BEACH EXCURSION
Crab footprints on the beach at Cape Leveque at sunset (Kimberley region.)
Journey with me through the naked landscapes of the real Australia.

Adam Monk

First published 2009 by Monk Art Photography
62 High Street
Fremantle WA 6160
Phone: (08) 9336 6102

Photography by Adam Monk
Text edited by Richard Ward, WA
Designed by John Douglass, Brown Cow Design, Fremantle, WA
Printed by Quality Press, WA
Scanning and image preparation by Adam Monk
Printed on Monza Recycled Satin by Spicers Paper
55% recycled, fsc certified

www.adammonk.com
info@adammonk.com

BREAKING WAVE
Rippling clear water laps the sweeping shore as far as the eye can see.
(Bremer Bay, South coast.)

the REAL AUSTRALIA

NAKED LANDSCAPES BY ADAM MONK

For my Mum , Denise, for showing me that almost anything is possible, and to my friend Rop Te Riet for teaching me how to 'see', all those years ago

CONTRAST

An ever-changing; ever-flowing pool. At the time of my visit, the countryside had just been ravaged by fire. After what was probably the most challenging drive in, over a road consisting of large boulders seemingly placed quite haphazardly, the gorge was a spectacular sight, contrasting with its black, bare surrounds. (Lennard Gorge, Kimberley region.)

Why the real Australia?

For me the real Australia is the Australia I know best, the Australia where I grew up and the Australia through which I have travelled extensively. It is the Australia I have seen most often, both with my eyes and through the lens of a camera. For me, this Australia is predominantly Western Australia.Therefore, for this book, although I have seen and photographed amazing places throughout the rest of the country, I have decided to focus on the places I know and love the best.

I have titled it The Real Australia because Western Australia's landscapes are more 'real' to me than anywhere else.

Western Australia is the least populated state of Australia, with most people living in the capital, Perth; so it's a place where you can find yourself alone – alone in places that remain untouched by human presence, as they would have been a thousand years before. Often, as I wander in the wilderness, I feel I am standing in a spot where no one has stood before.
Then I know I am seeing the 'real Australia'.

Why naked landscapes?

I have called these landscape images 'naked' because they are unclothed by human presence or influence.

Australia is one of the world's oldest continents, with some of the oldest rocks on our planet. Many of these rocks remain today as they have lain for the last four billion years, largely undisturbed by glacier movements, geothermal activities or other earthly grumblings that move rocks around, grind them into dust or otherwise alter the landscape. The rocks of Australia have had four billion years of erosion by wind, rain, sun and sea that has truly unclothed the landscape, exposing the bones of the earth – the ancient earth – in its truly naked form. Many parts of Western Australia reveal this nakedness in all its beauty, in all its harshness and in all its softness.

I believe the real art of my landscape photography is in capturing those elements and distilling them into a single image that conveys the feeling of actually being there.

My hope is that these images will give you a sense of my passion and love for these naked landscapes, so that my experience can be shared.

Adam Monk

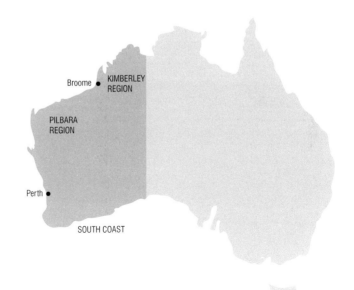

Broome • KIMBERLEY REGION

PILBARA REGION

Perth •

SOUTH COAST

RED FIRE (Previous page)
Red pindan cliffs reflect the setting sun. When the light had gone, I sat awhile and a pod of whales came close in shore to greet me. A magical moment. (Barred Creek, Kimberley region.)

FRACTURED ROCKS
Sunset over Two Peoples Bay Nature Reserve. The bay was named to mark a chance meeting of French and American mariners there in 1803. (South coast.)

LONGEVITY
The boab tree. A species with a flaky bark and spongy centre that can store over 100,000 litres of water. These unique trees stand for centuries – some say for over 1,000 years, but they have no growth rings to count, so no one really knows. (Near Derby, West Kimberley region.)

GLISTENING TWILIGHT
Waves lap peacefully on rocks they have polished for eons. (Thistle Cove, Cape Le Grand National Park, South coast.)

JOURNEY'S END
Timeless Antarctic waves arrive on shore. (Thistle Cove, Cape Le Grand National Park, South coast.)

STILL WATER. STILL WATCHER
A northern paper bark tree stands watch over Hamersley Gorge (Karijini National Park, Pilbara region.)

FOLDED TIME
Spectacularly coloured banded iron formations over two billion years old form dramatic outcrops in the Hamersley Gorge (Karijini National Park, Pilbara region.)

DAWN REFLECTIONS (Previous page)
If you arrive here at the right time of the day, you can have the whole place to yourself. This morning, when the light was clear and beautiful, and there was not a ripple of wind, I was in the gorge at dawn. I didn't see another soul for over three hours.
(Windjana Gorge, Windjana Gorge National Park, Kimberley region.)

NATURE'S PLUNGE POOL
Emma Falls rains down into an icy pool, while just a few metres out of picture is one of nature's warm springs. (Emma Gorge, El Questro Station, Kimberley region.)

PATIENCE
Mineral rich water bathes the base of Jofre Gorge. An international photographer, totally oblivious of my presence, walked into the gorge and sat down in the centre of this shot and had his lunch. I waited … and waited … (Jofre Gorge, Karijini National Park, Pilbara region.)

OASIS
A magical grotto amid a tiny remnant of Kimberley rainforest.
(El Questro Gorge, Kimberley region.)

PANDANUS REFLECTIONS
Pandanus palms shade a restful stop at Miners Pool on the rough and rugged Kalumburu Road on the way to the remote Mitchell Falls. (Drysdale River, Kimberley region.)

DISSOLVING LANDSCAPE
The Southern Ocean gently strokes the granite foreshore. Softly today;
savagely tomorrow. (Greens Pool, William Bay National Park, South coast.)

RIPPLING LIGHT
Two views of Madfish Bay at dawn. The waves at this beach come from two different directions. I wandered in pre-dawn light, in-shore and 50 metres out, where the waves barely lapped at my knees. It was so magical that I stayed there and managed to get sunburnt. (William Bay National Park, South coast.)

NATURE'S GIFT

The Basin at dawn. Mother Nature has caused the sea to create this calm, safe pool, fondly remembered by generations of Western Australian children.

(Rottnest Island, off the coast of Perth.)

SUMMER REMNANT
Sunset over a flawless white sand beach. (Parakeet Bay, Rottnest Island, off the coast of Perth.)

EARLY MORNING SWIM
Little Parakeet Bay. Here you may find more than just a 'naked landscape'. This is one of Perth's nude bathing beaches! (Rottnest Island, off the coast of Perth.)

GOD-LIGHT (Previous page)
The still quiet of the bay reflects the presence of gathering storm clouds. Clear emerald water is edged by white sand and smooth-domed rocks that stop the swell from reaching the shore. Sunset over Greens Pool. (Denmark, South coast.)

BONES OF THE SEA
Can you see? Across the transparent, dappled waters the ancient remains of a mythical sea creature seems to keep watch. (Twilight Cove, Esperance, South coast.)

WINDSWEPT
Painted grasses keep hold against moving sands under an uncertain sky in the Fitzgerald
River National Park. The park is a World Biosphere Reserve in which have been recorded
over 1,800 beautiful species of flowering plants – 62 of which are found only there.
(South coast.)

SANDSCAPE
Wind shapes a billion grains in the ever-changing landscape, where evening light reflects
the orange clouds at Beagle Bay dunes. (Kimberley region.)

RIPPLING VEIL
Flowing water reflects an iron-rich, rocky cliff. (Karijini National Park, Pilbara region.)

BURNT ORANGE REFLECTIONS
The Hamersley Falls at rest in the sunset afterglow, waiting for the big rains. (Hamersley Gorge, Karijini National Park, Pilbara region.)

OVER THE EDGE (Previous page)
Cobalt blues and rust reds contrast in the banded iron cliffs in this awesome gorge. (Hancock Gorge, Karijini National Park, Pilbara region.)

PRIMORDIAL AMPHITHEATRE
A very early morning experience as I had my breakfast with only the sounds of water and birds for company. (Jofre Falls, Karijini National Park, Pilbara region.)

KARIJINI NATIONAL PARK

I believe Karijini National Park is one of the wonders of the world. The sides of some of
the gorges are so sheer and so high, with the banded rocks, the pools, the trees and plants
painting the colours. No cathedral could ever reflect the creator more than this.

1.   A native spring flows from the gorge wall into Circular Pool.

2.   Water cascades into Regans Pool (Hancock Gorge).

3.   Dawn light reflected in Kalamina Gorge.

SOLE PRESENCE

As the sunlight faded rapidly from the red rock walls of Dales Gorge, the day visitors left me as the sole human witness to fiery red reflections in the plunge pool of Fortescue Falls. (Karijini National Park, Pilbara region.)

DAWN SNAPPY GUM
The slow-growing snappy gum is scattered throughout the Pilbara and Kimberley regions.
The stark white bark has a unique luminous quality, especially in the early dawn light.
(Mornington Station, Kimberley region.)

SLEEPING DRAGON
The crocodile-infested Pentecost River flows slowly past this prehistoric witness.
(El Questro Station, Kimberley region.)

BIRDSONG AT SUNSET (Previous page)

As I arrived at this remote spot on the Fitzroy River there was not a breath of wind. I was alone while what seemed to be thousands of birds shared the twilight moments with me. Never before had I been so serenaded, and never since.

MORNINGTON STATION
RETURN TO NATURE

Mornington Station is recognised as one of the last true wilderness areas.

The pastoral lease for the 312,000 hectares of the vast station has been purchased by the not-for-profit Australian Wildlife Conservancy and the lands are gradually being restored to pre-human intervention condition. The AWC acquires land and establishes sanctuaries for the conservation of ecosystems and threatened wildlife.

Mornington Station is a landscape of spectacular gorges, rugged ranges and tropical savannah. The vistas are dominated by the King Leopold Ranges and the mighty Fitzroy River. The Fitzroy and other rivers, such as the Adcock, Hann and Traine, slash the land with spectacular gorges.

It is a naturalist's paradise with 170 species of birds and much diverse wildlife, including several rare and threatened species.

Visitor programs promote awareness of the fragile nature of the environment and the need for vigilant attention to conservation.

The amazing vastness and beauty of Mornington Station's magnificent scenery took my breath away, leaving lasting impressions, which I feel privileged to share with you.

DEEP REFLECTIONS

A whole day's canoeing, but it was worth the paddling.
(Dimond Gorge, Mornington Station, Kimberley region.)

CROSSING OVER
In the Australian outback, you won't find many bridges. You just forge through the
water when it is shallow enough for safety. (Mornington Station, Kimberley region.)

SILENT SENTINEL (Previous page)
Lonely boab tree at sunset. (Mornington Station, Kimberley region.)

RED BLUFF
A sandstone promontory overlooks the Pentecost River, which flows below the
El Questro homestead. Formerly a cattle station, El Questro is now run as an
extraordinary wilderness experience, with a strong emphasis on nature conservation.

SHARP CONTRASTS
The hard, sparse landscape with its sharp rocky shoreline,
contrasts dramatically with extensive tidal flats that teem with
life. It has a unique beauty in the softness of the evening light.
(Cape Keraudren, Pilbara region.)

NO SURF TODAY
Looking towards Cape Naturaliste and a pink autumn twilight. This popular surfing beach was unusually calm.
(Leewin/Naturaliste National Park, South West region.)

SHIPWRECK COAST
A storm-lit sunset on the coastal sandstone cliffs of Kalbarri which, over several centuries have seen the doom of many ships and mariners.
(Kalbarri, Mid West region.)

PAINTED SKY
A moody sunset over the dunes of the Fitzgerald River National Park (South coast.)

APPROACHING STORM
Magical sunset colours reflect on the tranquil waters of Greens Pool. (William Bay National Park, South coast.)

THE SOUTH COAST

Some of the world's most beautiful beaches can be discovered along the south coast of Western Australia. The often changeable weather produces dramatic skyscapes that are particularly striking at sunset.

Secreted among an often craggy shoreline are sheltered bays and inlets where the smooth white sand squeaks between your toes and the waters are champagne clear. The small intimate beaches of the south contrast with the sweeping, endless stretches of the beaches of the north-west.

Tidal movements create wonderfully intricate patterns and evocative shapes in the sand.

1. **Melting chocolate.** Dawn at Lucky Bay.
    (Cape Le Grand National Park, South coast.)

2. **Dancing sunlight.** (Cape Arid National Park, South coast.)

3. **Liquid gold.** Thistle Cove (Cape Le Grand National Park, South coast.)

LONELY COAST (Following page)
Flamingo pink reflections on a Lucky Bay sunset as the waves retreat.
(Cape Le Grand National Park, South coast.)

AUTUMN TWILIGHT
The usually tempestuous waves around Sugarloaf Rock were stilled on this calm, windless autumn evening. (Near Margaret River, South West region.)

SUNSET WALK (Previous page)
Tidal Kimberley waters ebb and flow along this long sandy beach. Sunset over Cable Beach. (Kimberley region.)

EVENTIDE
Peach colours reflected at Point Ann, where the bay provides an annual nursery for whales and their calves. (Fitzgerald River National Park, South coast.)

ROCKY SHORE

Rocks weathered by millions of years of wave action. Just off this rocky shore is one of the world's natural wonders, Ningaloo Reef.

(Cape Range National Park, Pilbara region.)

GOLDEN LIGHTHOUSE
Day trippers leave the beach to the seagulls and me. (Pinky Beach, Rottnest Island, off the coast of Perth.)

IN THE DRY & BELL GORGE REFLECTIONS (2 images)
The Bell Gorge Falls cascade gently into the steep, deep gorge; but the waters will become
a wild, gushing cataract in the Wet season. (Bell Gorge, Kimberley region.)

SAFE HAVEN (Previous page)
A safe, calm environment for threatened marine life in this little-known, little-visited inlet.
Did you spot the fish? (Waychinicup National Park, South coast.)

BIRD'S EYE VIEW
The Murchison River flows slowly past Hawks Head Lookout as the
evening light reflects red off the ancient sandstone glistening after
recent rain. I could not escape the approaching rain front, but I kept
my camera dry. (Kalbarri National Park, Mid West region.)

FLAME POOL
The evening sun reflects from the rocks in this tiny remnant of water that was a rushing torrent in the wet season.
(Kalamina Gorge, Karijini National Park, Pilbara region.)

GREEN DEPTHS

A slippery walk through this narrow gorge is rewarded as the striated rocks lead you to this inviting natural pool known as Kermit's Pool. One toe in the water will convince you not to plunge in. It is mind-numbingly cold. Too cold for Kermit or any other frog! (Karijini National Park, Pilbara region.)

FLOWING PROMISE

The Fortescue River meanders and cascades over the rocks of Hamersley Gorge, creating small pools before flowing on to add to a beautiful swimming pool, bounded by awesome vertical cliffs.
(Karijini National Park, Pilbara region.)

WARM HAVEN

Hidden in dense tropical palms, a warm natural spring creates a series of thermal pools where the weary hiker (or photographer!) can relax and watch the butterflies. (Zebedee Springs, El Questro Station, Kimberley region.)

LIQUID SILVER
Water flows from fractured rock in Hamersley Gorge.
"… shall we bring water for you out of this rock?"
(Numbers 20:10). (Karijini National Park, Pilbara region.)

RIPPLED REFLECTIONS
At the end of a long day in Hamersley Gorge, I was freshened
and revived by the beauty of the light on the surface of this pool.
(Karijini National Park, Pilbara region.)

BAND OF BEAUTY

Ferns cling to towering cliffs around this pristine pool. The sight will take your breath away, as can the frigid waters for those hardy enough to swim.

(Circular Pool, Karijini National Park, Pilbara region.)

HIDDEN JEWEL

The waters of the Fortescue River feed into the most perfect natural swimming spot in the Karijini National Park – a hidden jewel.

(Fern Pool, Karijini National Park, Pilbara region.)

DAWN MEDITATIONS
The rising sun reflects the ochre rocks and verdant banks with their paperbark trees and Pandanus Palms. (Barnett River Gorge, Kimberley region.)

SHEER REFLECTIONS
Sunset at Windjana Gorge. "No one can see their reflection in running water. It is only in still water that we can see." (Taoist proverb)
(Windjana Gorge National Park, Kimberley region.)

AWAKENING VALLEY (Previous page)
Mornings in the Pilbara can be bitingly cold. I was up and walking before the first light of dawn gradually shedding layers of clothing as I warmed up and the landscape steamed around me. It was worth the effort! Even the hard rocks seem as alive as the trees and bushes when softened by the dawn light.
(Dales Gorge, Karijini National Park, Pilbara region.)

RUGGED FRONTIER
The Pilbara's vast ancient plains and red gorges have their own rugged appeal and a special beauty. (Pilbara region.)

FAMILY GATHERING
A grove of boab trees of varying ages. According to local Aboriginal legend, when the boab grew to maturity its flowers were mediocre and its fruit had a bad odour. The Tree Spirit became so angry that he yanked the Boab out of the ground and replaced it in the earth upside down. The Australian boab tree is closely related to the African baobab tree. African bushmen have a legend that the tree was thrown from heaven and landed upside down. Dr David Livingstone described it as 'a giant upturned carrot'.
(Near Derby, West Kimberley region.)

CROCODILE COUNTRY
The mighty Pentecost River, home to huge, unfriendly crocodiles, and the much sought after barramundi fish, flows to the tidal waters of the Cambridge Gulf in the far north of Western Australia. The river is often the beginning or the end of a great adventure for many travellers and this crossing is a milestone for those who travel the rugged Gibb River Road. The sign warns the unwary visitor against swimming here. (Kimberley region.)

PENTECOST DAWN (Page 88 - 89)
Early morning light reflects the clouds
over the still waters of the Pentecost River.
I slept on the roof of my car, awakened
sporadically by large splashing sounds. As
I set up my camera in the morning, I spent
much time looking over my shoulder – the
crocs here can be up to five metres long.
I realised that in this spot I was no longer
'top of the food chain', but potentially
an appetising dinner for a prehistoric
monster. It was so hot that I kept cool by
taking water from the river in a bucket and
tipping it over my head. As appealing as
the river looked, that was as near as I got
to swimming.

IN THE BEGINNING … (Previous page)
The timeless, weathered bones of the
ancient earth and the luminous spinifex
grasses bathe in the light of a painted
evening sky. (Karijini National Park,
Pilbara region.)

RED DAY'S END
As the sun sinks over the junction of the
Timor Sea and the Indian Ocean, the red
pindan cliffs seem to glow from within.
(Cape Leveque, Kimberley region.)

STEPPING STONES
A tea-coloured steam flows into this hidden cove under a southern winter sky. (Norman's Inlet, South coast.)

SILENT WATERS
Massive boulders lie as if scattered by a giant's hand in this sheltered inlet, where the beauty is such that I didn't know what to photograph first. (Waychinicup National Park, South coast.)

BEAUTIFUL HEAVEN
The inaptly named Hellfire Bay is actually one the most beautiful beaches in Western Australia, with clean white sands and unusually worn rocks to investigate. (Cape Le Grand National Park, South coast)

FARAWAY CASCADES
Worth it when you get there. Travel east from Derby on the Gibb River Road for many days, then tackle the bone-shaking Kalumburu Road with nine inch high corrugations, before turning left on the track to Mitchell Plateau for another day. When you think the road couldn't get any worse, pull into the Mitchell Plateau campsite for sleep. Get up at first light, walk for about 3 hours carrying a heavy camera bag, and then … aaahhh! That's why I came …
(Mitchell Falls, Kimberley region.)

SUMMER WATERS (Previous page)
The reclining rock on the shoreline of this popular holiday island seems to point the way to the famous *City of York* wreck site some 200 metres off shore in seven metres of water. The *City of York* sailed from San Francisco to Fremantle and sank when it struck a reef (July 12, 1899) just 12 miles from its destination. Eleven of the crew, including the captain perished. (City of York Bay, Rottnest Island, off the coast of Perth.)

Photographic Philosophy

I am a landscape photographer because I love the natural world and its wild places: Landscape photography is a passion for me because it gives me a medium to respond to nature, and the ability to share it with others.

The mechanics of the photographic medium have become second nature for me. I am able to control the technical side accurately without thought, and concentrate on the image itself, trying to transmit what I am experiencing within the bounds of the camera viewfinder. Even when I'm rushing to catch that fading light, I'm watching, listening and feeling everything at once, being a part of it. Then it's almost like breathing in the light and the landscape, and exhaling the image.

I've been passionate about the natural environment since I was a very young. I spent most of my childhood holidays camping in and around Western Australia's South West, exploring forest tracks and finding beautiful secluded spots to set up camp and be in amongst the natural beauty.

There were no toilets or facilities, rarely was anybody else there, just the birds, kangaroos and lizards. I was about 14 when I stayed in my first "public campsite" with my family. The site had gas BBQs, toilet facilities and cold water showers… I remember thinking 'this isn't camping… what are we doing?'

These days I do stay in public campsites when I can't avoid it, such as National Parks or places that are on private property, but my quest, as always, is for that isolated place, far from the influence and evidence of human intervention.

Sometimes that just means getting up before everybody else, having those couple of hours of the pre-dawn and dawn to myself, or heading out when most others are returning to camp, catching the sunset and that elusive twilight in breathtaking spots, with nobody else around. These times leave me speechless and awed by the majesty of the natural world. At these times of day the true colours are visible, the subtle ones that the sunlight washes away. At these times there is no glare, no black shadows and the heat has softened. At sunset it's like the whole land breathes a sigh of relief, while at sunrise it's doing its stretches ready to start the day.

TECHNICAL

For all the images in this book and indeed my gallery, I have used 2 cameras: a Fuji 6x17 large format Panoramic, and a Rolleiflex 6x6 medium format. Both of these cameras use a large piece of film for each shot, ensuring maximum resolution and clarity of images. Until recently this still exceeded the best digital had to offer… that is changing rapidly and I am looking forward to trying out some new equipment.

THE EXPERIENCE

My aim is to show the majesty of nature as you have never seen it before, not in a way that is unrealistic, but so realistic you forget to breathe for a moment. I want these images to be something you will never get tired of, something that is timeless and eternal.

I invite you to come into my Gallery at 62 High St, Fremantle in Western Australia, where the whole range of "the Real Australia" is on display in all its naked glory. Printed as large limited edition art works my images truly become windows into these ancient landscapes, windows that transform any home or office, bringing with them that wonderful sense of peace and tranquillity.

If coming to the gallery is impractical then please visit my website www.adammonk.com. The site contains a comprehensive choice of my works and is intuitive and simple to navigate. When you have made your choice there is a fully secure purchase facility through PayPal, ensuring your private details go no further, and I insure and ship worldwide directly to your door.

ACKNOWLEDGEMENTS

There are many people who have helped a great deal in the completion of this book, I would specifically like to thank, Steve and Pam Reynolds, for their invaluable input on the original concept and planning. John Douglass of Brown Cow Design, for his great layout and design skills and patiently going through all my revisions and alterations without complaint. Nigel & Ruth Goodman, my business partners and friends, for their support and encouragement over the years. My friend and colleague, Greg Hocking for so generously giving of his hard earned knowledge and experience.

The Department of Environment and Conservation (DEC), for doing such a great job of maintaining the many wonderful, diverse and often remote National Parks in Western Australia, and of course all my friends and family, without whom, none of this would be worthwhile.